A Rainbow
OF OUR LIFE

A RAINBOW OF OUR LIFE

iUniverse books may be ordered through booksellers or by contacting:

iUniverse
1663 Liberty Drive
Bloomington, IN 47403
www.iuniverse.com
1-800-Authors (1-800-288-4677)

Because of the dynamic nature of the Internet, any web addresses or links contained in this book may have changed since publication and may no longer be valid. The views expressed in this work are solely those of the author and do not necessarily reflect the views of the publisher, and the publisher hereby disclaims any responsibility for them.

ISBN: 978-1-5320-6343-5 (sc)
ISBN: 978-1-5320-6344-2 (e)

Library of Congress Control Number: 2018914292

Print information available on the last page.

iUniverse rev. date: 01/02/2019

A Rainbow of Our Life

ELENI VOYAGES

$\mathcal{A}$ GUEST AT MY DOOR

You enter my home
With a halo on your head
You come as a guest
But I want you to stay.

You make my home sacred
When you enter through the door,
You came as a guest,
But I want you to stay.

As you enter through my door,
You bless my heart, you bless my soul.
You take away my pain.
You came as a guest,
But I want you to stay.

****

ANGEL IN DISGUISE

Thank you for giving me,
That ultimate moment in my life
The moment that cannot be replaced
With any other

Thank you for giving me.
The forever sunshine, the rainbow
The fire, that will forever burn.

Thank you for giving me my first grandchild,
For that angel in disguise
Will mend my broken heart,
My soul and my life

****

COLORS

Baby Pink and Baby Blue
They are both so different
And yet so much alike,
The Blue, a rainbow on the sky,
My life's most precious moments.
My Gemini.

The Pink, a sunset on the sky,
So serine and so fine
I wish it lasts forever
And that's my Libra, oh so just.

The Pink, the Blue,
Both so gracious and so pure,
Together, they pave my path,
With the stars and the moon,
And yes, some clouds are there too.

****

AMILY

The time has come
To leave the negative behind
And start anew with family in mind,
Because my darlings,
Family is the ultimate thing.
Without it you don't exist.

So renew your vows,
Which are rooted in your hearts.
And aim *kardia mou (my heart),*
To have your own,
Before you grow, to be too old

And your bearing years,
Will reach the end,
And you'll be left without an heir
To carry on your name

****

GENESIS

I was planted in your soul
Where I started to grow,
And in your heart, where I've learned to dream,
Where I've been taught to love,
I will love you forever.

However, an instant approached to move forward,
Planting, seeds of my own
And while leaving my heart behind,
I will love you forever,
I will love you forever

****

$\mathcal{G}$IVE ME THE MARKS

Give me the marks,
That cover your body.
Give me the noir that shadows your beauty,
And let your body shine.

My desire to blow away the darkness,
And make your body shine,
Is greater than the distance
From this planet and beyond

I dream of a miracle,
With faith, prayer and hope,
A miracle that can turn your negative into mine,
And let your body shine.

Give me the marks,
That covers your body.
Give me the noir that shadows your beauty.
And let your body shine.

****

I HOPE AND PRAY

Your passing came so fast,
Although you've been in bed so much.
It was so hard for us to accept that fact
Especially for me
For I chose to close my eyes.

Self sacrifice would not have been enough
To truly prove what was in my heart
And now you're gone.

I wish to God
I had another chance,
To tell you both how much I hurt,
And ask for your forgiveness,
As well as time to repent.

I hope and pray
When my time is up,
My soul will fly to where you are.

****

I'M 50 AND I'M PROUD

I lived on mountains and riverbanks,
I played with goats and sheep,
Until I came to cross the ocean,
And found myself on city streets.

There were blacks, and there were whites,
And others with funny eyes
And everyone spoke a funny tongue.
I went through bridges, tunnels and such.
I earned my wrinkles and hunch back.

I heard commotions,
I felt excitements, but now,
With pains and aches, my life is crowded,
On the horizon I see a cloud,
But, so what I'm 50 and I'm proud.

****

I SMILE WHEN I THINK OF YOU

(From a MOM to a CHILD on Mother's Day)

I smile when I think of you.
Your bubbly personality,
Your humor and your honesty.
You are my angel, my laughter and my tears.

I laugh when you come around,
When you tell me crazy things,
Although on times we don't agree,
I appreciate your honesty.

There are times when you bring me tears,
But that's what makes us both complete.
I lived to be my age,
Because you are part of me.

When I smile, when I laugh, and even when I cry,
It's all because of you,
Because you see my angel,
Life is not all laughter, it also has some grief.

Thank you for picking me to be your MOM
And giving me one more chance to celebrate this day
To laugh, to smile and shed a happy tear
The fact that we are together
It makes it worth the deal

****

IVING WILL

Before the years ahead of me, will fade away
Before my health will leave me limp
For your sake my love
I want to go.

I want you to remember me,
As I am today,
My intentions are not
To cause you pain.

I don't want to become a burden,
In fact, that is what I want to avoid
I want to release you, from deciding my fate.
I don't want to be a load.
I just want to go

****

MY SWEET ANGEL

My Sweet Angel
I love you so
Your sparkling eyes,
Your one million smile,
Resembling the stars
My sweet angel
I love you so.

My sweet angel
I love you so.
Without you, I'm all alone.
You give me life,
You give me hope.
My sweet angel
I love you so.

****

PRETTY LADY ON THE RUN

She moved around so freely,
Smiling like the whole world belong to her
A pretty lady on the run,
She seemed to have much fun

She run, she laughed, she loved,
But her life was not complete,
For she had not become a MOM,
A pretty lady on the run

The day had finally arrived,
In June of '69,
The pretty lady had a child,
Her son, now was her world,
She ceased to exist,
She put her life on hold

As the years went by,
She loved him more and more,
And all the wealth and treasures,
From this planet and beyond
Cannot precede the love she felt,
Each time she saw him smile.

****

REMEMBERING THE FAIRYTALES

Remembering the fairytales
You told us through our lives.
Remembering the lullabies.

Sitting around the fireplace,
With my siblings by my side,
Remembering the fairytales
You told us through our lives.

Although a little child,
Sitting on your lap
I remember you, singing lullabies.

I remember you by my side,
In good times and in bad,
Wiping away my tears, but most of all,
I remember you singing lullabies.

****

SHORT TEMPER

(Condition of the Human Race)

Is it something buried deep inside?
Is it something far beyond the soul and the heart?
Is it HURT and BITTERNESS?
That you can't CONTROL?

I'm bitter and I'm hurt,
But I don't kick and I don't strike.
I don't push against the wall,
I have a soul and a heart
I have control.

I don't ever curse, I don't even judge.
I have a soul and a heart
I have self respect, and respect for all.
I have control.

****

SPRINGTIME

Light – Love - Unity

The sun is rising early in the morning
The days are brisk and awaking
Birds are singing
Flowers are blooming.

Strolling down a path,
Paved with petals of the most exotic flowers,
The air is filled with a mixture of scents.
Lilies, and Roses, Lavender and Honeysuckles

Springtime the loveliest of the season
When all things come alive
Springtime is the resurrection of the Universe,
The resurrection of all God's creations

****

SUDDEN STORM

On a brisk winter day
Chatting the hours away,
Pleasant moments, humming thoughts,
For the newest bundle of joy

With laughs and smiles
With faith and hope
Appending the twig
That's been missing from the tree.

Suddenly came a winter storm.
Which snatched away, my Christmas Joy
Along with it, it took my heart,
To shatter once again...

****

THANKSGIVING PRAYER

I thank you God
For everything you've given me.
My health, my children
And my family.

I thank you God
For all the feelings and emotions
But most of all, I thank you God,
For answering my prayers,
And once again
You brought my family together.

****

THE INVISIBLE ME

Your eyes are looking straight at me,
But your soul is blind
And you can't see.
The invisible me.

Your being is walking right through me,
But your heart is made of steal
And so, the crash you can't feel.
The invisible me.

I am sitting on the couch,
Right there by your side
You make me feel so eerie,
The invisible me.

Can't make you aware,
Though my existence is not that far,
Your soul is blind, and you can't see.
The invisible me.

****

THE ROUND TABLE

Low, round table
Placed in a small corner of the room,
Grey, cool, misty like climate in a whole,
Platters of food placed on it,
All, round and small.

One more I said,
One more for all to enjoy,
But there are only few of us,
Just three or four.

Moving like a turtle,
In a slow motion way,
Waiting, waiting still, for all to come,
Sad, so sad.

Strange, so strange,
No one is there…,
But something woke me up.
Tears on my pillow
Tears in my eyes.

****

THE STARS ABOVE ARE SHINING

Raising my eyes to heaven
With a prayer in my heart,
Hoping for the moment, you'll arrive,
To lift me up!

The stars above are shining
And telling me you're on your way.
That day will be
My greatest thrill,
For you will fulfill my dream.

****

TODAY'S CHILD

Because of who I am I can forgive
Can you guess of who I am?

Because of who I am I can forgive,
Each time you slap my face
I turn the other cheek.
Can you guess of who I am?

Because of who I am I can forgive.
Each time you tie my hands behind my back,
Each time I'm forced to kneel.
Can you guess of who I am?

Each time you put a knife
Right through my loving heart,
I become stronger. I survive
Because I know one day,
Your child will break your heart
And I want to be there to gently pick it up.

Because of who I am, I can forgive
Can you guess of who I am?

****

TREASURES

The treasures in our life,
Are the little things that count
Deep into our heart.

The cry of a little child,
The laughter of an old man's senile smile,
Or maybe the young man's broken heart.
The treasures in our life,
Are the little things that count.

There are many things surrounding us,
Micro or extravagant,
Such as the beauty that seems to catch our eye,
But tell me my darling,
Can that also capture our heart?

Refrain

The cry of a little child,
And the old man's senile smile,
As well as the young man's broken heart,
Are the treasures in our life.

****

THE TIME IS NOW

If you are ever going to love me,
Love me now, while I can feel
The sweet and tender feelings,
Which from true affection flow.
Love me now
While I am living.

Do not wait until I'm gone
And then, have it engraved on marble.
Sweet words on ice-cold stone.
If you have tender thoughts of me,
Please tell me now.

If you wait until I am sleeping,
Never to awaken,
There will be death between us,
And I'll be unable to hear you then.
So, if you love me, just a bit,
Let me know while am living.

AITING

(Mona Lisa)

Waiting forever, to come my way,
That precious gift of God,
Each time and every day,
When I look into your eyes
I hope to see a shining star,
And a Mona Lisa smile.

****

Printed in the United States
By Bookmasters